Ode to Beautiful

poems by

Sandra Sidman Larson

Finishing Line Press
Georgetown, Kentucky

Ode to Beautiful

This book is dedicated to:

My parents, Eleanor and Gordon Sidman,
who introduced me to the sea; and

my grandmother and grandfather, Bessie and Charles Newmiller,
whose house in Misquamicut, Rhode Island, provided a summer
home for our family when I was just an infant, until it was washed
away in the great hurricane of September, 1938; and

the tides of life that have washed these loved ones away, leaving my
sister Shirley Hogan and I to walk the beaches with our loving
memories and gaze out to the distant horizon.

ACKNOWLEDGMENTS

Grateful acknowledgement is made to the editors and readers of the following
publications where these poems, or earlier versions of them, have appeared.

"Rock Fever," *Chaminade Literary Review,* Volume 12 & 13, 1993.
"Hawaiian Roots," *Hawaii Pacific Review,*
  http://hawaiipacificreview.org/2014/06/12/seeds/#more-744.
"Ode to Beautiful" and "Pearl Divers," *Pudding Magazine,* #62 2014.
"Five Mile Long Red Ribbon: Reflections on a Tal Streeter Installation
  Surrounded by Kites at the Weisman Museum of Art," *River Poets Journal,*
  Lilly Press, Spring/Summer 2012.
"A Faint Perfume" and "Between Worlds," *Southwest Journal,* August 1997.
"Asbury Park," *Southwest Journal,* Summer 1991.
"A Girl's Instruction for Body Surfing," "Small Worlds of Blue," "Asbury Park", and
  "Jersey Argonauts," Over a Threshold of Roots, *Pudding House Press,* 2007.

I would especially like to thank Leslie Matton Flynn for skillfully helping me improve this
manuscript, preparing it for publication, and my other fellow Foreword group members:
Jim Bettendorf, Stephanie Brown, Barbara Draper, Susan Crouse, Kristin Laurel, Ardie
Medina, LeRoy Sorensen, Miriam Weinstein, and William Upjohn. The support and
suggestions they have given me over the years has improved my craft in general and many
of the poems in this manuscript in particular. I also owe a deep sense of gratitude to Jude
Nutter and Thomas R. Smith, two wonderfully skilled and dedicated poets, who, as the
mentors of the Foreword program and as friends, have guided me, and our circle, for
many years. Also thanks to Roseann Lloyd, my first poetry teacher and long time mentor
who also assisted with this manuscript.

Publisher: Leah Maines
Editor: Christen Kincaid
Cover Art: Sandra Sidman Larson
Author Photo: James Henry Larson
Cover Design: Elizabeth Maines

Printed in the USA on acid-free paper.
Order online: www.finishinglinepress.com
        also available on amazon.com

Author inquiries and mail orders:
Finishing Line Press
P. O. Box 1626
Georgetown, Kentucky 40324
U. S. A.

Table of Contents

Before Hawaii

Sixteen hundred years ago,
Polynesians, navigating the unknown,
sailed past their understanding

and found these flowered islands,
that lay beyond the reach of any
other land on earth.

In double-hulled canoes they came,
crammed in among taro plants,
breadfruit trees and tapa mats,

waking and sleeping among pigs
and small dogs, they drank the juice
of coconuts and cracked open

a new world
that flourished for a time.

Section I

Inner Pearl Surfaces

*"But the sea
which no one tends
is also a garden"*

William Carlos Williams

Ode to Beautiful

Opaque water tells
of my granddaughter's small neglect
as I switch on the tank light.

I drop a few grains of flaked food
onto the water's surface and watch
its slow rotating descent.

Beautiful, a sliver of a fish, appears
from behind miniature mottled rocks.
Even in the murky water, she glows,

her mouth silently forming
a small "O"—open to what
such a tiny pebble

of consciousness can swallow,
in what will be her brief
swim through life.

Do Not Disturb

1.
A seal rests on his side
just beyond the tide's reach,
belly facing the surf.

The hide of his tapered body is sea-glass
smooth and the sheen on his fur has a hint
of green cast by algae.

He stirs and rolls his four hundred pounds
as if to take me in, exposing a flank

and face dabbled with sand
a mouth decorated with a fountain
of whiskers that waver when he breathes.

His wide-set eyes, half-closed,
open as I greet him. I give him
a wide berth for solitude, for rest.

2.
When the ancient Polynesians
first saw these seals,
snouts in the air, struggling

like their dogs,
to leave the surf,
they named them

ilio-holo ika uaua
(dog who runs in rough water)

3.
And the ancient *kahunas* spoke
in a magical tongue allowing them to learn
the seals' land-bound history, how

they craved a saltwater home,
and how the gods, half-granting their wishes,
turned their limbs to fins.

Now these seals can swim for miles,
but they must surface for air,
find rest on shore.

And who is to say what the true origin
of this story is or how they were named?
This history has washed away.

4.
Now we call them Hawaiian Monk Seals,
for they do have short brown hair and a cowl
of skin that drapes around their neck;

monkish ways as well as they travel
unaccompanied through cathedrals
of sea-space, passing alcoves of atolls.

They dive deep and hold
their inhalations like yogis.

5.
The seals probably would prefer to rest
in an un-peopled place, but these colonized
islands are an outpost of their old home.

These days, mostly sad things wash up—
spent fuel drums, Styrofoam cups, condoms,
Q-tips, piles of plastic trash, yet

we are happy to see the seals. At least here,
they are safely out of the shark's reach
and the deadly web of fishermen's nets.

This beach in Kapaa on the windward side
of Kauai is a place I also come after a long journey,
a place for solitude, for rest.

6.
The beach narrows, and I turn back, thinking
of cleaner shores when I was a wave-
leaping girl. I see the seal, still asleep, but his plot

has changed. Brass stanchions looped with red
velvet ropes are anchored into the sand and
on one a hotel placard swings, commands,

DO NOT DISTURB

7.
But these seas are warming,
breeding toxins that leach
the reefs a ghostly white.

A deadly stillness rests over
these forests, diminishing,
the teeming life a seal needs to survive.

Is extinction after thirteen million years
of survival to be his future? I want
to reassure the seal, tell him,

*We too want to continue living
in this blue, watery world.
We can stop the heat from rising.*

Silent for a moment, I realize
I can't say what he most needs
to hear—

*and we will do it now,
and we will do it soon enough
to save you, to save us all.*

If only I could hang this placard
on doors all over this loud
world's trampled hallways.

DO NOT DISTURB

DO NOT DISTURB

A Girl's Instructions for Body Surfing

Like a seal
                    nose up—
Swim swiftly
        through the chaos—
                    land and water
                colliding—
Swim
        into deeper water—
Eye
        the horizon—
                its distant spine—
Watch
            the water's undulations—
        its shifts
                of mood—
                    a huge wall
            forming
                from uneven weight
Do not flinch
        Stroke quickly
                through an arc of
        pure stillness
                and light—
Turn
        Plunge forward—
                    Join the wave's force—
                falling
                    falling—
        your ears' shells
                    echoing the loud roil—
Ride these sea shoulders—
                    girl
                    Cling to
        your father's neck—

Ride into
                    the vortex of what's next.

Between Worlds

On silent slants
       of parrotfish, I slip

down an iridescent chain
       of being.

A dash of orange
       surrounds

the precise eye
       of a squirrelfish

who examines me,
       but darkly.

Black-fingered sea urchins
       beckon like

Baba Yaga bending down
       from her house on stilts.

Through streets of rainbow
       wrasses

jaywalking
       this way and that,

I swim with
       with hands outstretched,

forming
       a Buddhist greeting.

Clouds of light
       pass through

the silver throngs
        above.

My heart
        sounds in my ears.

Sea-plumed hair waves off
        other life

darting through
        breathing coral reefs.

Kicking,
        leaving behind shimmering fish,

I surface
        into an indifferent world

that lacks a precise eye to see,
        or be beckoned by,

a world
        that may not survive.

Pearl Divers
The Sea Ranch, California

Below steeply stepped cliffs, the rocking Pacific
stills into emerald pools. Seaweed patches drift

on the calming swells, along with other enigmatic
figures. As they emerge from the watery confusion,

I see they are young men in wetsuits and snorkels,
each carrying what looks like a crowbar and a pail

leaking sea water. By prying the abalones' feet
from the rocks they have captured these

endangered creatures. Assembled on the sand,
they survey this loot. Their reward will be selling

what should not be bought or sold. I want to climb
down the cliff and tell these greedy dreamers:

Let the abalone survive. Weigh the worth
of the inner pearl surfaces of your own lives.

Rock Fever
Hilo, Hawaii

Pele, Goddess of fire,

heaves. Her volcanic anger

reddens the sky,

forms stone rivers

that follow their own force

to the sea. Her lava oozes

over livelihoods, moves

silently, plows

over the rush

of an island risen

from Her mouth—

before men in outriggers first gazed

at the fixed star,

before these islands were pirated

by lesser gods—

entrepreneurs whose schemes

She still displaces

if it pleases Her.

As it does today.

New Rituals Needed

Nighttime off the coast of the island of Hawaii

A molten river of lava bursts
from underground, oozes
over the land incinerating

scrawny trees, exploding
low-lying structures. A passenger
on deck beside me whispers,

> *Can you believe this?*
> *Can you believe this?*

as the luminous lava plunges
over the cliffs, roiling the surface
of the sea, which hisses as it splits.

Sulfurous winds blow
in our direction. Our Hawaiian host
offers this chant,

> *E Pele e Pele   ka uka ulï ana*
> *E Pele e Pele   hua ina hua ina*

Moving through the warming waters,
moving along with a culture constrained
by islands, we do not sing songs

as if we too were land-bound.
We do not comprehend these words,
and yet we do understand them.

Smoke wafts through his words.
The chanting done,
another passenger speaks up,

> *The whole world is heating up,*
> *and, we don't even have a prayer.*

Only the smoke-filled wind responds.

Time's Tide

Words and phrases are from Rachel Carson's The Edge of the Sea, but not necessarily in the order they appear in the book.

The sea's edge   strange
                elusive
Patterns shaped
          by intermingle and overlap

The sky full of dawn
             apricot color
Water incoming
         surging surf

Sand spheres   Only the hardy survive

Sea life forms
              Confused tumult of sounds
swashings
         swirlings   murmurings
and whisperings
         Restive waters

Echoes living creatures seeking
           foothold

Teeming life   An uneasy sense
            of universal truth
Inscrutable
        Just beyond
our grasp

A world where man is
       uneasy

So mutable the tide
      A world apart

The sea's unifying   touch

            Its lambent sheen

Section II

Silvered by Sea Water

"We are like islands in the sea, separate on the surface, but connected in the deep."

William James

Five-Mile Long Red Ribbon: Reflections on a Tal Streeter Installation Surrounded by Kites at the Weisman Museum of Art, Minneapolis, Minnesota

An image shoots up out of sleep.
It may be the flight of a kite's red ribbon
and answers will rise in the clear weather of sleep.
Chances to run are finite, so take this chance and run.

It may be the flight of a kite's red ribbon,
so crane your neck to the sky, run with your dreams.
Chances to run are finite, so take this chance and run.
Desire is a string that feels like flight,

so crane your neck to the sky, run with your dreams.
How far does the wind run?
Desire is a string that feels like flight.
What can't be followed or caught is found in sleep.

And how far does the wind run?
In art childhood may be reclaimed,
and what can't be followed or caught is found in sleep.
Now that childhood has flown, we are left the future.

Yet in art, childhood may be reclaimed
and a kite can be remembered by the feel of a red ribbon.
Now that childhood has flown we are left the future.
If only the space of the sky were the length of childhood.

A kite can be remembered by the feel of a red ribbon,
and how brief and how long a kite string, a childhood, a dream.
If only the space of the sky were the length of childhood.
Hold on to the red ribbon, don't stop. Run, run!

How brief and how long a kite string, a childhood, a dream.
Answers will rise in the clear weather of sleep.
Hold on to the red ribbon. Don't stop. Run. Run!
An image shoots up out of sleep.

Small Worlds of Blue

circled our cottage door in summer
when blue hydrangeas bloomed,
and blue greeted me everywhere.

Cresting sand dunes, wind whipping
my towel into leggings, I saw a blue line stretched
so it had to curve to stay on earth.

Tugged skyward by the taut, unreeling string,
I followed my box kite as it rose, swooped into blue,
and when it fell, I flung it again

into the morning wind. Bayside
by afternoon, balanced on snail-coated rocks,
I netted blue-shell crabs, held them

at arm's length as Father had taught me,
and, on my way home, listened to their claws
scratching against the inside of my pail.

Evenings, on the screened porch reading
by a lamp set on a table with wobbly legs,
I was side by side with Nancy Drew.

In her blue roadster, we were independent
girls, driving into the curve of mystery.
After bedtime prayers, I remember distant trains

whistling, always whistling on a straight line
to somewhere curved, somewhere beyond
our cottage, the blue hydrangeas.

Asbury Park, New Jersey, 1955
For J.C.

Sand slows the pace of two
teenagers walking on the beach,
their edgy talk accompanied
by pounding surf. Finally they reach
the wooden steps of the boardwalk.

They move into the false
glare of lights, cranked up music
from a sound system drowning
out the pounding sounds of surf.

At the shooting gallery, he places
a coin on the counter, takes
careful aim at her desires,
winning her an over-stuffed bear.

The night deepens,
the teenagers move on
through a double-clutch of evening
under the rhinestone stars.

With his convertible top down,
they sit in swirling distances,
a small light the only guard
in the hallway of her house.

They touch tongues
over cotton-candied teeth.
Each breath they take sounds like
the miniature oceans they are.

Jersey Argonauts

A young girl again, running to the beach,
I'm watching sunrise-silhouetted fishermen leap
from bloody waters pulling
        fish-filled boats to shore.

They unload piles of mackerel. Gills stilled
by useless air; the dead fish begin to stink. Listen!
Crying—
        seagulls circling.

Salt-sweating, silvered with fish slippings,
jeweled by sea water, the silent fishermen
        glisten in their work.

My water breaking, I cry out,
riding waves rising, falling. With one last surge
I expel you, slippery,
        onto this shore.

You begin to pump your lungs, breathe
this ocean of air.
I listen to
        your gull-like cry.

Silvered by sea water you are alive,
shining, and I
        am brilliant in this work.

Rain in Kaneohe
Hawaii

1
In the garden, after the jungle light
has crushed the gardenias white,

smeared their fragrance across the lanai,
I hear the sea stirring.

Trumpet vines blow along the fence,
scraping banana leaves

agitate as the wind grows louder.
I open a small diary and words

spill out in a voice I've never heard.
I have opened a secret that doesn't include me.

Soon, rain rushes up the mountain,
falls back, the soil bleeding red.

Rain on the roof so loud
nothing said can be heard.

2
Now, I move among the soft swish
of pines and maples,

but when the wind blows my hair
and I feel the storm coming,

I hear the tropical rain
as it rushes up the mountain

and falls back. I smell gardenias
and step again into that first garden,

so often soaked in silence,
and listen for reassurance after rain.

Parking One Night Under the Pali
Kaneohe, Oahu, Hawaii

I turn off the headlights, open
the windows, and feel the wind
as it wanders about in the night.

Dark mountains, like drapes pulled shut,
loom above me, hiding my darker
fears. Once they were here—

armies clashing high on the Pali. Pushed
over the precipice, the warriors leapt
into air—and death on the rocks below.

Tonight, only the rising moon and my dreams
troop across the silent cliffs.
No trace of them.

Such cruelties in a land nourished
by rain, in a land wrapped in brilliant
feather cloaks, in a land pierced by infidelity,

birds, and shocking flowers. If you listen,
say with a shell pressed to your ear,
you can almost hear screams suspended in air.

Hawaiian Roots

I walk by a garden pool
where water lilies drift

with afternoon reflections,
showing off their creamy faces.

Once in a fit of rage I tore
the alamanda vines I'd grown

off my backyard fence.
Someone else lives there now

and they may have trellised
new flowers on the fence. *So beautiful,*

what can't be seen by others.
On certain afternoons

when reveries grow green and
the wind off the Pali arrives

forcing me to lean into it,
I still want to open the gate,

survey what flowers there now,
but I will leave others to prune

what is best pruned back.

A Visit with My Youngest Son Who Lives in Kauai

The shores of your childhood reappear,
as this plane sinks toward land, and I remember
I hadn't studied the distance of children
before you were born. How I sobbed

at the side of your crib, and wondered how
to raise you. How I took you by the hand
and walked you to school. How I left you there
to learn of paradise.

Your letters have brought me here,
long on explanation. You don't greet me
with a flower lei. You say you carry
flowers in your heart for me.

Winding through bougainvillea groves
on our way to your home from Hanapepe,
we eat at King Kung's in Kapaa.
What cannot be reclaimed fades into night.

You say I never spoke enough of love,
yet when you were a boy I sewed
Hawaiian shirts and shorts for you and picked
the ilima flower with buds small and hard

as passion, it's white and waxy leaves
used for wedding leis. What is said
in Hawaiian is not what is meant.
If I had learned to speak the language

I would have needed only vowels to talk
of love. I know one has to speak softly here.

The next night I buy a dress, pink and yellow
with hibiscus flowers, only $19.95
at K Mart. We dine in an old sugar mill,
beside a small fountain where red gingers bloom,

and a pool where small blue fish dart about.
We try to separate sunset from evening.
I'm thirsty for the sounds of gardens. I believe in
the savage taste of flowers, and yet you are the one

living here. Why is paradise so far from home?
We visit the seven *heiaus* along the Wailua River.
They say ancient Hawaiians wander near
at night among the koa trees.

The *mana* here is the most powerful on the island,
and you are helping to build a temple in this place.
I say, *You can't count on anything quite like this,*
even though you were born here;

I'm building on very old lava, you say.
My thoughts turn to what is consumed by fire.
On the road from Kapaa to the airport in Lihui
we're headed to the gates of Aloha Airlines.

The road, crooked with construction, the rumble
of soil-red trucks buries our words. At the gate,
we hold our embrace for a long moment,
now our words are muffled by the roar of engines.

I wave *Aloha* from the small window, my long
explanations beside me. I look to see the
flowers. I will write to tell you I love you
and I can only hope you believe me too.

I had wanted to bring my own gifts to you
to speak with an open heart, to heal
the bruises of distance, our misunderstandings,
to offer you the flowers of my long life.

Blessings

1.
I get a letter from an old lover as the crabapple trees bloom,
more dazzling this spring than I can remember,

the new leaves glisten after last night's rain, the air
seasoned with morning. I think how idle I was

in my youth. No concern for what time would do,
all the petals full-blossomed, enduring.

2.
It's hard not to be aware of desire even if
it should leave the body,

yet it will never leave the heart,
or if the heart, never the memory.

Today I am thinking about it—
the muscles that tensed and held on.

To turn flank to flank, feel nipples
flare and fine hairs rise to hum like a tuning fork;

the subtle music of sound vibrating
to the breath of the other: I am thinking about this.

3.
I remember a night flight to Puerto Rico
where middle-aged men began to swarm,

bringing me perfume and invitations to their high rooms.
To have such power one hasn't earned on one's own

is to be so surprised, so very alone. José was the bellboy,
about my age, with a smile and tropical blue eyes

like the nearby sea, and he had fine-tuned muscles, and English
enough to help me try to put soul and passion together.

I was after the wings
of desire, the spirit of fire,

the casting
of flesh into love. But

I got only to the edge of my desire;
body to body touching,

the surf smoothing
the friction of skin on skin.

4.
Here in the snow of the falling blossoms,
I think of them as blessings.

When the French say *blessure* they mean wounds,
and I follow that thought while

the trees keep dropping their petals,
and I continue to catch and to hold them.

Dining Out
St. Thomas, U.S. Virgin Islands

I can't hear what she is saying,
the skinny nut-brown woman

in a baggy yellow bikini
sitting on the patio as the sun

subsides, the hurricane lanterns
become more visible, as darkening

palm fronds lean in to the small tables
of this outdoor restaurant, and the waves

whisper about their relentless task
wearing down the reefs. Her skin

looks as if it were withered by water,
and the man in fluorescent bathing trunks,

with his own weathered look,
covers her hands with his.

I'm so hungry
I order for two.

Rafting on the Jungle River in Costa Rica My Friend Loved
In memory of Elizabeth West

I feel a steadying touch on my arm.
In this jeweled land
my friend's loving absence

breathes beside me. So much
morphine in her last months,
drifting in and out of sleep,

in and out of sentences,
when she spoke to me
only in her mind.

She said Buddhism wasn't
warm enough: She wanted
a Christian burial.

We drift, with dripping paddles
raised, through slow flowing water
and float into a cathedral of green

dense canopy— where toucans
torch the quiet overriding the songs
of unseen birds and a waterfall

spills into the river casting
a misty veil over us
as we step from our raft.

Here in the jungle,
the ceremony mine,
I wrap her gently

with large, gleaming leaves
and leave her in a simple,
emerald cave.

This Tropic Death Laced with Cinnamon
Fort Lauderdale, Florida
In memory of my father A. Gordon Sidman Jr.

In the intensive care unit,
between your short,
shallow breaths,
you reminded me how,
when I was a child,
my friends called mother
Mrs. Cinnamon, not
Mrs. Sidman, our family name.
Why did you think of this
just then, seasoned
with a coppice of needles,
lying white in your flavorless bed?
And why, that evening
before re-entering the hospital,
as the sun anointed the sky red,
did I call out *Cinnamon*,
as if making an offering,
as the day shifted
from evening
to night and your death
the next day?

Fleeting Ecstasy

In memory of my mother and father and their home in
Deerfield Beach, Florida

Palm trees with unbraided hair dance
to the drumming wind, welcoming afternoon arrivals.

An umbrella snaps in the wind and under it, a sun-scorched
girl squats, attentive to her father and a sandcastle

as he builds it for her, tier by tier, then drops
a ball at the top. It winds in and out of passageways,

a mystery of what is seen, what isn't. The waves wash
up on the beach, wash back. Wash up, wash back,

leaving a sparkling train of silver and holes
that open for an instant, filled with tiny prey

that excite sandpipers, which in sideward, psychedelic
motion, try to snatch, like all of us, what disappears

too soon. Beyond the edge of the churning sea, ready
to execute their next move, boys suspended

on surfboards face the teeth of incoming waves, swivel,
raise their arms to embrace their power. Soon the golden rays

of the setting sun splay out across the darkening day,
turning the sea a scarlet shade of red, and the gulls

quiet, finally having little to say.

A Proper Ending
Sian Ka'an Biosphere Reserve, Yucatan, Mexico

A dead jellyfish tumbles within the tide's reach,
translucent mantel collapsed, its tendrils swaying

like rain in wind confusion. Each wave advances it;
each wave a pallbearer moving toward shore.

A crab, mounted on eight short legs, scuttles by,
sidestepping my questions of why.

The fronds of palm trees—gills for the tropical air—
breathe in, breathe out, rustle in the breeze.

These forms, this flight, these shadows, this light
place me on a surface of calm

where, with my toes, I begin to inscribe
lines on the sand in circular form,

a mandala completed
only when vanished with the tide.

A Faint Perfume

When comets first spawned
we were their afterglow
and salmon sang in the sea

now their brilliance flashes
for a moment on the surface
of the rushing river,

then below in deeper shades
and with the passing
of each moon

time begins
its soundless escape from desire
as salmon struggle

upstream remembering
their way back home
a faint perfume

is all they have
to go on.

Notes

Do Not Disturb

Hawaiian Monk Seal, ilio-holo-ika uaua (ee-lee-o holo ee ka ooa-ooa) The endemic Hawaiian monk seal is critically endangered and headed toward extinction. The Marine Conservation Biology Institute, Hawaii, reports approximately 1,100 remain in the wild.

Kahunas were the priests or sacred instructors in ancient Hawaii. Now the word may mean any teacher of wisdom.

Pearl Divers

Abalone are cold water snails that are endangered because of their desirable meat and iridescent inner shell. Washington State prohibits their taking. In Northern California some limited fishing is permitted.

Rock Fever and New Rituals Are Needed

In Hawaiian tradition Pele is the goddess of fire, lightning, dance, volcanoes and violence. Given the volcanic activity in Kilauea, a mountain on the island of Hawaii, Pele's is thought to spend time there.

Private parties and tourist boats go out at night when the lava is flowing to watch the spectacular fall of the red hot lava into the ocean.

These first two lines of a longer chant translate roughly as:
> *Oh Pele, Oh Pele, moving along*
> *Oh Pele, Oh Pele, bursting forth*

Time's Tide

This poem consists of words and phrases taken semi-randomly from Rachel Carson's book *The Edge of the Sea* published by Houghton Mifflin Company, Boston and New York, 1955.

Parking Under the Pali
Pali means *cliff*. Nu'uanu Pali Lookout is the most famous in Hawaii. Located on the windward side of Oahu where King Kamehameha I, in 1795, attempting to unite all the island using his huge army, drove hundreds of local warriors over the cliff to their death 1,000 feet below. Some say on certain nights the screams of falling warriors can still be heard.

Hawaiian Roots
While standing behind a woman in the grocery store I heard: "So beautiful, what can't be seen by others."

A Visit to My Youngest Son Who Lives in Kauai
Heiaus are old Hawaiian temples and *mana* has many meanings, one is spiritual power.

This poem was written just before 9/11 in the days when one could walk to the airline gate with departing quests.

Sandra Sidman Larson holds a Bachelor of Arts degree from the University of Minnesota and a Master's of Social Work degree from the University of Maryland with a concentration in community organizing and planning. She managed and led nonprofit organizations focused on social justice, social service, and management support throughout her career.

Sandra traces her life path branching into writing, as opposed to only reading poetry, when she took a class at the Loft Literary Center of Minneapolis in 1985. She has continued to study the art, and was chosen in 2010 to participate in a two-year program, for manuscript development at the Loft Literary Center, later renamed as *The Foreword Program*. She continues to meet with a group of 11 students from this program, and, in 2012 she and eight of her fellow Foreword participants published an anthology of their poems titled *Gatherings*.

Sandra has lived in the Twin Cities since 1972. Her poetry appears nationally and internationally in journals, magazines, anthologies, and on various poetry websites. Naomi Shihab Nye nominated Sandra for a Pushcart Prize in 1999 and she was also nominated for a Pushcart Prize in 2012 by Carolyn Harris Zukowski, editor of the *Literary Bohemian* for a poem written in the form of tweets. Much of her published poetry can be found at her website http://www.cardinalpointspoetry.com.

Three chapbooks other than this current one, comprise her published manuscripts. With her new full-length manuscript, *This Distance in My Hands*, Sandra was a finalist for the Lost Horse Press' Idaho Prize for Poetry (2013), Trio House Press Trio Award (2014) and the Main Street Rag Press Poetry contest (2016). This manuscript will be published by Main Street Rag Press in 2016.

www.ingramcontent.com/pod-product-compliance
Lightning Source LLC
LaVergne TN
LVHW091233080426
835509LV00009B/1265